PENGUIN MO[...]

The Penguin Mod[...] [...]s
and diversity of [...] *gs*
together representative selections from the work of ..... ts,
allowing the curious reader and the seasoned lover of poetry to
encounter the most exciting voices of our moment.

ROWAN EVANS is a poet, composer and sound artist born in 1991, who studied at Cambridge and Bristol universities. He is the author of *returnsongs* (Wide Range, 2012), *freak red* (Projective Industries, 2015), *ODE RHIZOME MOUNTAIN SONG* (Moot Press, 2016) and *cante jondo mixtape* (If a Leaf Falls Press, 2017). Rowan composes music and sound for performance, theatre, film and installation and is artistic co-director of the interdisciplinary performance company Fen. He co-edits Moot Press and co-curates the Anathema reading series. In 2015 he received an Eric Gregory Award from the Society of Authors.

Widely considered the greatest living poet in the English language before his death in 2016, SIR GEOFFREY HILL was born in 1932 to a working-class Worcestershire family. He studied at the University of Oxford before going on to lecture at the University of Leeds, the University of Cambridge and, from 1988, Boston University, where in 2000 he co-founded the Editorial Institute with Sir Christopher Ricks. His poetry books include *For the Unfallen* (1959), *King Log* (1968), *Mercian Hymns* (1971), *Tenebrae* (1978), *The Mystery of the Charity of Charles Péguy* (1983), *Canaan* (1998), *The Triumph of Love* (1999), *Speech! Speech!* (2000), *The Orchards of Syon* (2002), *Scenes from Comus* (2005), *Without Title* (2006), *Selected Poems* (Penguin, 2006), *A Treatise of Civil Power* (Penguin, 2007) and *Broken Hierarchies: Poems 1952–2012* (OUP, 2013). He received numerous awards for his work, including the Eric Gregory Award, the Whitbread Award for

Poetry, the Faber Memorial Prize, the Hawthornden Prize and the Truman Capote Award for Literary Criticism. He served as Professor of Poetry at Oxford from 2010 to 2015, and was knighted in 2012. This selection was made with Sir Geoffrey, with the assistance of Kenneth Haynes, between December 2015 and April 2016.

TOBY MARTINEZ DE LAS RIVAS was born in 1978 and grew up in Somerset before studying history and archaeology at Durham. He first worked as an archaeologist, and this, together with the landscape of Northumberland and the work of north-eastern writers such as Barry MacSweeney and Gillian Allnutt, has had a significant impact on the development of his own poetry. He won an Eric Gregory award in 2005, the Andrew Waterhouse award from New Writing North in 2008 and the Newcastle Australia Residency Award in 2013. A pamphlet of his work was published by Faber as part of the Faber New Poets scheme in 2009; his debut collection, *Terror*, was published in 2014, and his second, *Black Sun*, in 2018.

MODERN POETS 7

These Hard and Shining Things

Rowan Evans

Geoffrey Hill

Toby Martinez de las Rivas

PENGUIN BOOKS

PENGUIN BOOKS

UK | USA | Canada | Ireland | Australia
India | New Zealand | South Africa

Penguin Books is part of the Penguin Random House group of companies
whose addresses can be found at global.penguinrandomhouse.com

Penguin
Random House
UK

This collection first published 2018
001

Poems by Rowan Evans copyright © Rowan Evans 2012, 2015, 2018
Poems by Geoffrey Hill copyright © Geoffrey Hill 1959, 1968, 1983, 1998, 2000, 2002, 2005, 2006, 2007, 2011, 2012, 2013
Poems by Toby Martinez de las Rivas copyright © Toby Martinez de las Rivas 2014, 2018

The moral right of the authors has been asserted

Set in Warnock Pro 9.65/12.75 pt
Typeset by Jouve (UK), Milton Keynes
Printed and bound in Great Britain by Clays Ltd, Elcograf S.p.A.

A CIP catalogue record for this book is available from the British Library

ISBN: 978-0-141-98782-8

www.greenpenguin.co.uk

Penguin Random House is committed to a sustainable future for our business, our readers and our planet. This book is made from Forest Stewardship Council® certified paper.

CONTENTS

ROWAN EVANS

rains	3
A METHOD, A PATH	5
wulf ode	9
ERRATICS	10
from *cante jondo mixtape*	12
Envoys	15
from *WULF*	21
freak red	25
Stems (1)	29
Stems (2)	31
from *15:44*	32
charm / vision	36

GEOFFREY HILL

The Turtle Dove	39
Ovid in the Third Reich	40
September Song	41
from Four Poems Regarding the Endurance of Poets	42
from The Songbook of Sebastian Arrurruz	43
from *The Mystery of the Charity of Charles Péguy*	44
from *The Triumph of Love*	49

from *Speech! Speech!*	52
from *The Orchards of Syon*	54
from *Scenes from Comus*	58
Improvisations for Jimi Hendrix	61
from In the Valley of the Arrow	64
from *Pindarics*	66
Citations I	67
from In Memoriam: Gillian Rose	68
from *The Daybooks I: Expostulations on the Volcano*	71
from *The Daybooks II: Liber Illustrium Virorum*	74
from *The Daybooks III: Oraclau ǀ Oracles*	76
from *The Daybooks V: Odi Barbare*	77
from *The Daybooks VI: Al Tempo de' Tremuoti*	79

TOBY MARTINEZ DE LAS RIVAS

Twenty-One Prayers for Weak or Fabulous Things	85
Three Illustrations from *Blake's Europe: A Prophecy*	90
Poem, Three Weeks After Conception	92
Things I Have Loved	94
Blackdown Song	95
Père	96
Untitled	97
Testament	98

Misereatur	99
Woodbury	100
Hurry	100
(clouds)	101
from *Black Sun*	102
Hunting Kestrel, Danebury	103
Intimate Portrait I/for S. N.	104
To a Metropolitan Poet	105
Diptych: At Matfen / Address to my Daughter	106
Crucifixion with Dragonfly	107
Crucifixion, August, Lullington	108
from Titan/All Is Still	109
Acknowledgements	117

Rowan Evans

rains

& tenser falls

puncturing
firwood as before

              in ancient
              -ness o

myth if

        stationed
        subkiss

would sing
my weight in

                pollen

rain looked
nude to

            toucheth hills

        they smoke

whereas ground
worried blush at O

        if where water
        was   *could be*
            here

(quadrant stone who
 yields you silvers)

      why then,
      wet spoker

in the whole earth's afternoon

A METHOD, A PATH

'Ive stood nor seen them till they flew away'
 – *John Clare, who responds*

my field is piebald; i no longer disciple myself to the visible, bearing as if toward the tower. ghosted in the total locality of the flurry, the white parts of birds. of the poem. holding it balled in my hand, the air is cold enough that snow doesn't melt, but compacts. now writing is like this snow. too much compaction, the hard kernel lacks air to buoy itself. it must be lain again with air – snow spreading into prose

sub-spring clots each foot with intentional dark. there is a tremble: rivulet poses out of a wilde broken water-table, subsuming hoof, consuming with the river itself. and by this gesture shows that substance may rise through permeable ground; and by this how right we are to wait; and that waiting is a verb defined by spring. this course of becoming unmute, re-met and breathing as a lapse in pressure allows it so: now *they* are coursing through the scrub as well as *thee*, telos and anterior,
o many-antlered wet

again a nearby makes us still, moving only as much to empt, to match, a slowing flit of the head. so our voicings halt and drop; and so our subjects coagulate to this one: *again, robin*. in token of beckoning, succumb. the flick, a hush. still, remember how the others would treat us, the acceleration –

and re-enter the poem, so i might startle it into showing itself. writing is disruption owing to its presence. and must. one shows a green back – yellow – drawing – gone (that other copse of name and clatter), what i've come to collect nor datum nor song (now this kindling digress, now this). violence, hallowed as this violence upon myself. so speak: I have seen the nape of my works in retreat

wulf ode

(for Barry MacSweeney)

too far now
from plover sound & starres

my dock-town is
leafed print.

good friend avoid & braid
a highway
of yr breath

(oils leapt &
offering)

for the sea grapes turn

for blue these stickle
annexes of verse

ERRATICS

ERRATIC behaviour | thrown-up and carried by | strength of circumstance | Yes | this force of happening | act as shrapnel to | but also this | long wait since deposit in a place | otherwise unchosen | anomaly in rift | behave erratically and remain stubborn | on the spot you're thrown to | until obstruction resembles accepted fact | the age will split mid-colour | my anger is erratic | so what's done will sit in open field | until such time as I begin to ask | how it came here | what passage wounded it | fallen against the burgeoning storm-beach of the unwritten thing | hence

    ERRARE
    ,errs,
      the night errand is
        to stray
blind, according to a slow trail, I stray, intending to stray, and trust
        the ethic of the force
          but these stones
            are tidal

sea's driven over grass
that is hair in the crotch

brushed by falling water | and one half of a kiss floats above | EROTIC shore | what's erotic is | wanting a body | not having it | the rock assembles mass from the dying glacier that carries | but can't keep it | I am shivering in the wake of your pleistocene | and sisyphus, heretic, loves the rock | but won't hold it long enough at the peak | to carve a nude | can't fuck the rock | so gratefully I accept this wrenched block of metaphoric stone | insisting in its error it is here | so real it has to be avoided

from *cante jondo mixtape*

orange blossom

he must record the light
in columns
over the epitome.

atrium of a lake

death of Lorca

>	/

in the diminishing acoustic
white cracked walls
of the mission courtyard.

full breaths over the mountain
half breaths lain in heat

oranges.

the acoustic
diminishing.

>	/

his mouth.
a sodden cloth in his mouth

ink and vinegar.

waking in white stations
sending into them
vows.

something he wouldn't imagine
in other brickery
in other words

hard, brown, Andalucía.
olive, green, Andalucía.

/

a second light in the gorge.

dangerous little walkaway.

ask him, is he thirsty.

yes, those are flamingoes.

/

the brown mare
looks at the white egret.

if he could smile.

for a moment
the tower is everything

swifts above *the innocents*

swifts swifts

south-trending
tower!

    /

beauty overbore me

so much movement in it.
if i had a voice
of math

(only he
must record the light
only this
orange blossom)

said the virgin
said the mudéjar
this would be the spring
of algebra

Envoys

The holly flecked with song and alarum.
Deft the holly, flaying wind with leather
arcs of the tongue. And I am leveled, bound
to choose or dart as
              [*oikos*] 'the body
is not *in* space, it inhabits space',
intelligent water now reaming in
a diademic cold.

What I wouldn't call communion
of the senses, ochre clefts truant
from the spreeing words, and too much Latin
snared in the bog where thorns bud yellow.
Gorse pushing between pools on the moor
states only in aspect, abject glimmer,
something unfelt but said.

Sunlight is alien technology
geared to loosing agency over
the stone beaches of Inis Mór.
Metal in a low rain, more of the ground
and clad to it than light is. Turned
to face the fixed descent, phasing with sleep,
I pledge myself onto external things.

Reading the elegy that winter is,
moonlight caught in a runnel at the close
edge of the field, in every other rut
on the flooded clay.
A quality of apprehension
itself, not of the object lit upon;
light | ictus | falling on the backs of stones.

Prone in its silence is the sea. *Not yet,*
abeyance is a dark and shuttered room.
The sea already there, completed by
[*what is this pause*] intermittence:
subject in relation to wave.
                                        'The sound
you hear is the sea' where light fails; all
signals primed, switching on.

Darkness from when. The plane of this world
'is wholly contingent with a body',
and those are words remote from night-flare.

In a yellow light, certain tracks pass
the submerged reeds and blackish water of
the Hackney Marshes, where I've never been.

from **WULF**

Extracts from an adaption of the Anglo-Saxon poem 'Wulf and Eadwacer' created by Fen, an interdisciplinary collaboration based in Bristol. WULF combines choreography, bilingual poetry and an original score with field recordings made at Avalon Marshes, Somerset, and adapts one of only two surviving poems in Anglo-Saxon to be written from a female perspective. In performance, the text is spoken by two Chorus voices which correspond to the left and right columns, and by a central figure (italics) who speaks in Anglo-Saxon.

Contemporary English speakers may find that the meaning of certain words is aided by reading aloud. The letters 'þ' and 'ð' both sound as 'th'.

EDGELAND

Sindon wælrēowe

send in the blood-hungry

                    send in the eager

the troop

                    on þrēat

meet threat with threat

                    at morning

mark an edge

                    ǣt morgen

sharpen sightlines
þonne we

                    hit the waste

þonne we

                    mark the track

Wulf is on īege,   ic on ōþerre.
Fæst is þæt ēglond,   fenne biworpen.

island to island

                                      ēglond to edgeland

blade-edge pitched
toward fæstland
hours of running

                                      keeping up

gangan

                                      keeping up

cwic wē cumað

                                      in force

we cumað

Sindon wælrēowe   weras þǣr on īge
willað hȳ hine āþecgan,   gif hē on þrēat cymeð.

                                      quick, head up
                                      we come ond gangaþ

drawn into circle
by edges of sight

                                      a break in cover

and snatch at space

                                      edge in, edge out

ond brecaþ for cover

                    Ungelice is ūs

WULFHEAD

Gehȳrest þū, Ēadwacer?   Uncerne earmne hwelp
bireð wulf tō wuda

wolf of the wood
fenland wælgast
we name it þine

                      gather arms, gear and wæpnum

over bounds
and far from ēglond

                      a mark on his head
                      a blade at his back

swā swā

                      the blamed-one

swā swā

                      the wolfhead

so so the war-pack
will stalk the outer rim

now watch ahead

                      now watch the wood

bearing harm toward us

DEADMŌNATH

in the deadmōnath

                              the wolfmonth

in the sickmonth

                              hrīmcold

here lyth our londes
poles and walkers

                              scarred from peat
                              in drowned pits

þǣr we standaþ
þǣr we mac shelter

                              black coppice dimlight

naked āctree, wintramōnath

                              the deadtime
                              the wūlfmonth

coldflōd taken all our londes

                              wætre beflowen

and in the dark, all is enemy

freak red

'fœðisk frekr í skógi' – *Old Norse rune song*

'. . . had a whole damn wood
in them days'
   – *Ian Hamilton Finlay,* Glasgow Beasts

   1

not in the wood where claw
covers gills & shards of cambium,
archangel at my tooth door
& bluebell pools like thought

   2

if could smell likethis
       rrr rr ffff f fbeserk
on haunch like sex like
this whole waking
i love! glade arc still
anyhow you're sleeping
longtimes
        under me

   3

is how you feel on
a street after some
bloody moon flick
      ,dark
doing that *thing* to space

is a sack no
dog no bladehead

    4

mid oath street
  hearing only
moon whos

                    „kv rr " rʳ
      comin

    5

is how you feel shitbins mmm
borders running vulpine
thru & up &
down the place
                    not just
                round it
mm   yr house,
a pastime between two
    empires of toadflax

    6

liberty & free movement
between the polis & the wood,
what *is* that
                we'll have
had reasons &
chronicles, civic *as*

animal & walls
        rabid with toadflax

7

sleekit,
        reynard,
out in yr garden where i'm
doing not much hard

8

some significance
  or none if   heh
the bark the dagger
you sent
toned upward, in
question heheh
        carnadine,
not in
  the horror genre

9

these are the liberties
these the robust sentences
of pissing our language that's
clearer
        over here

   ,where

                here

10

a thrush on
a syringe sings

    'easier to
blame someone with
four legs' mmm
    my back sloping
is the third line
      of every other riddle

11

maybe the totem of
night, death
& beauty is
a blackwood throat
    placed in front
of yr chest
& barking,
    maybe

12

& how to the sons
& daughters of
campion
    you scream
i shudder to think
  o freak red
  in public

Stems (1)

THERE IS THE CULTURE OF GESTURES
>O erasure, cloud hackle
>forced over head. Is it
>valid to be temporary
>in a drop, carving
>sound from here.
>Who says 'opal green'
>still hating so many?

EFFIGIES YARDS HIGH, SUDDEN CHANGES OF LIGHT
>Total non-engagement
>now not possible, and
>how to write. Beauty is
>a warrant for constriction
>and word 'ours'. White
>gravel, little rabbit bone,
>the sun today is shattering.

MODULATIONS OF TENSION, LEVEL BY LEVEL
>Into damaged fields
>before acquaintance we are
>directly aware, in the
>hour of vision. A blast
>steals the light and dark
>pattern of a bank in
>this refulgent summer.

ARRESTED IN FLIGHT AT SOME POINT
>Our cities with glowing
>hand kept safe, no rain
>that's nice. Heat delivered
>rapidly to surrounding areas,
>transparent garments.
>So far as experience extends
>there are no exceptions.

A SERIES OF COMPRESSIONS, SCENIC FRICTIONS
    Shudder in the next room
    as if this could make peace
    commissioned by the blaze.
    On foot and noun-heavy
    they are lit this afternoon,
    interminable. At corners
    pillars stand gold, empty.
OTHER SIMPLE DIRECT MOVEMENTS

Stems (2)

First appeal of linkages
signed onto absence
    where
    bright-lit
flower in lowland purely
human & now haunted
    revolves
    each way.
Errors are frequent &
embedded in the idiom
    serve to
    account
for periods of activity
pro-rosea, stalks of red
    become
    glad mesh.
Limbs falter on clearest
channels (one word won't)
    car of
    amaryllis
that machine translation
striking anti-pose with
    arms or
    embers.
Project to fall from,
heavenly disc is useless
    hung in
    view &
fronds from the white
stone make no allowance,
    the cast
    basilica.

from 15:44

III

The trace in the monitors
was undeniable and mirrored
no one living in our station.

An entry chamber panelled
with tools and icons, its dimensions
approximate to day
and burning optimum.

Bones and empties are void
or have no visible geometry.
Mesh without vortex, curves
un-extruded
            How total in
a glade of future habit, our rage
plumes empty

                                  The dead and hyper-real

Control in opposition

                                  Senseless presence

To an echo of former motion

                                  For, For,

The body translated

                                  With, From

And the spiritual body

                        It was agreed we had mistaken
                            one blue icon for another,
                                reverting hands to a
                                star less repeatable.

                        By the time our voices had been
                                converted to mesh
                          the shape had grown terrible
                                in their potential.

The sea falling away
in unsure cloaking

                                I wait for it to load
                                counting portents,
                            fearful of my position

An ocean revealed to those
who lag in magnetic winter

                                cannot press your face
                            into the side of a phantom

o metroid plates commanding light

                                you cannot, cannot,
                                light forms a body
                                but is only light

that flesh could be
succeeded by a judder
more violent than chrome

                                        when it reveals itself,
                                        glass pteron of black,
                                        our hope tilting in
                                        the dark corona

give up the body
counting hells, *aornos*
'place of no birds'

                             I begin at keyframe 1 and end
                             at 40, the motion between latent
                             with fear of not returning

speaking out on speculation

It does not respond

                                        When I am no longer vivid

It does not respond

                                     Now awful and manifest
                                   finding itself unrestricted
                                   and flexing in display

That the body could be

                                     sings multiple with blades

The process succeeds in advancing
my trace over the cusp, I dread the tint
of weightless fuselage

                                                                   'multifoliate rose'

'and sightless, perpetual star'

                                                                   had not expected this

When I am no longer vivid
my voice will enter the chamber
Where my body cannot
and look upon its face
rendering creed and supplication

	toward	from		with		below	
at	**waning**		past		beside		since
	under	into		for		**arc**	
before	against	**body**		among		via	
	without	above		by		over	
in	**judder**		off		within	**light**	
	after	of		**temple**		outside	

charm

the river is spread like a five-point goatskin

others see kingfishers when they are with him

vision

'for beauty is nothing / but beginning of terror'

I am on my knees in the fritillary bed

Geoffrey Hill

The Turtle Dove

Love that drained her drained him she'd loved, though each
For the other's sake forged passion upon speech,
Bore their close days through sufferance towards night
Where she at length grasped sleep and he lay quiet

As though needing no questions, now, to guess
What her secreting heart could not well hide.
He caught her face flinched in half-sleep at his side.
Yet she, by day, modelled her real distress,

Poised, turned her cheek to the attending world
Of children and intriguers and the old;
Conversed freely, exercised, was admired,
Being strong to dazzle. All this she endured

To affront him. He watched her rough grief work
Under the formed surface of habit. She spoke
Like one long undeceived but she was hurt.
She denied more love, yet her starved eyes caught

His, devouring, at times. Then, as one self-dared,
She went to him, plied there; like a furious dove
Bore down with visitations of such love
As his lithe, fathoming heart absorbed and buried.

Ovid in the Third Reich

'non peccat, quaecumque potest peccasse negare,
  solaque famosam culpa professa facit.'
  – Amores, *III, xiv*

I love my work and my children. God
Is distant, difficult. Things happen.
Too near the ancient troughs of blood
Innocence is no earthly weapon.

I have learned one thing: not to look down
So much upon the damned. They, in their sphere,
Harmonize strangely with the divine
Love. I, in mine, celebrate the love-choir.

September Song

born 19.6.32 – deported 24.9.42

Undesirable you may have been, untouchable
you were not. Not forgotten
or passed over at the proper time.

As estimated, you died. Things marched,
sufficient, to that end.
Just so much Zyklon and leather, patented
terror, so many routine cries.

(I have made
an elegy for myself it
is true)

September fattens on vines. Roses
flake from the wall. The smoke
of harmless fires drifts to my eyes.

This is plenty. This is more than enough.

from Four Poems Regarding the Endurance of Poets

TRISTIA: 1891–1938

A Valediction to Osip Mandelstam

Difficult friend, I would have preferred
You to them. The dead keep their sealed lives
And again I am too late. Too late
The salutes, dust-clouds and brazen cries.

Images rear from desolation
Like ruins upon a plain.
A few men glare at their hands; others
Grovel for food in the roadside field.

Tragedy takes all under regard.
It will not touch us but it is there –
Flawless, insatiate – hard summer sky
Feasting on this, reaching its own end.

from **The Songbook of Sebastian Arrurruz**

COPLAS

i

'One cannot lose what one has not possessed.'
So much for that abrasive gem.
I can lose what I want. I want you.

ii

Oh my dear one, I shall grieve for you
For the rest of my life with slightly
Varying cadence, oh my dear one.

iii

Half-mocking the half-truth, I note
'The wild brevity of sensual love'.
I am shaken, even by that.

iv

It is to him I write, it is to her
I speak in contained silence. Will they be touched
By the unfamiliar passion between them?

from *The Mystery of the Charity of Charles Péguy*

1

Crack of a starting-pistol. Jean Jaurès
dies in a wine-puddle. Who or what stares
through the café-window crêped in powder-smoke?
The bill for the new farce reads *Sleepers Awake*.

History commands the stage wielding a toy gun,
rehearsing another scene. It has raged so before,
countless times; and will do, countless times more,
in the guise of supreme clown, dire tragedian.

In Brutus' name martyr and mountebank
ghost Caesar's ghost, his wounds of air and ink
painlessly sprouting. Jaurès' blood lies stiff
on menu-card, shirt-front and handkerchief.

Did Péguy kill Jaurès? Did he incite
the assassin? Must men stand by what they write
as by their camp-beds or their weaponry
or shell-shocked comrades while they sag and cry?

Would Péguy answer – stubbornly on guard
among the *Cahiers*, with his army cape
and steely pince-nez and his hermit's beard,
brooding on conscience and embattled hope?

Truth's pedagogue, braving an entrenched class
of fools and scoundrels, children of the world,
his eyes caged and hostile behind glass –
still Péguy said that Hope is a little child.

Violent contrariety of men and days; calm
juddery bombardment of a silent film
showing such things: its canvas slashed with rain
and St Elmo's fire. Victory of the machine!

The brisk celluloid clatters through the gate;
the cortège of the century dances in the street;
and over and over the jolly cartoon
armies of France go reeling towards Verdun.

2

Rage and regret are tireless to explain
strategems of the out-manoeuvred man,
the charge and counter-charge. You know the drill,
raw veteran, poet with the head of a bull.

Footslogger of genius, skirmisher with grace
and ill-luck, sentinel of the sacrifice,
without vantage of vanity, though mortal-proud,
defend your first position to the last word.

. . . . . .

4

This world is different, belongs to them –
the lords of limit and of contumely.
It matters little whether you go tamely
or with rage and defiance to your doom.

This is your enemies' country which they took
in the small hours an age before you woke,
went to the window, saw the mist-hewn
statues of the lean kine emerge at dawn.

Outflanked again, too bad! You still have pride,
haggard obliquities: those that take remorse
and the contempt of others for a muse,
bound to the alexandrine as to the *Code*

Napoléon. Thus the bereaved soul returns
upon itself, grows resolute at chess,
in war-games hurling dice of immense loss
into the breach; thus punitively mourns.

This is no old Beauce manoir that you keep
but the rue de la Sorbonne, the cramped shop,
its unsold *Cahiers* built like barricades,
its fierce disciples, disciplines and feuds,

the camelot-cry of 'sticks!' As Tharaud says,
'all through your life the sound of broken glass.'
So much for Jaurès murdered in cold pique
by some vexed shadow of the belle époque,

some guignol strutting at the window-frame.
But what of you, Péguy, who came to 'exult',
to be called 'wolfish' by your friends? The guilt
belongs to time; and you must leave on time.

Jaurès was killed blindly, yet with reason:
'let us have drums to beat down his great voice.'
So you spoke to the blood. So, you have risen
above all that and fallen flat on your face

5

among the beetroots, where we are constrained
to leave you sleeping and to step aside
from the fleshed bayonets, the fusillade
of red-rimmed smoke like stubble being burned;

to turn away and contemplate the working
of the radical soul – instinct, intelligence,
memory, call it what you will – waking
into the foreboding of its inheritance,

its landscape and inner domain; images
of earth and grace . . .

6

            . . . No wonder why
we fall to violence out of apathy,
redeemed by falling and restored to grace
beyond the dreams of mystic avarice.

But who are 'we', since history is law,
clad in our skins of silver, steel and hide,
or in our rags, with rotten teeth askew,
heroes or knaves as Clio shall decide?

'We' are crucified Pilate, Caiaphas
in his thin soutane and Judas with the face
of a man who has drunk wormwood. We come
back empty-handed from Jerusalem

counting our blessings, honestly admire
the wrath of the peacemakers, for example
Christ driving the money-changers from the temple,
applaud the Roman steadiness under fire.

We are the occasional just men who sit
in gaunt self-judgement on their self-defeat,
the élite hermits, secret orators
of an old faith devoted to new wars.

We are 'embusqués', having no wounds to show
save from the thorns, ecstatic at such pain.
Once more the truth advances; and again
the metaphors of blood begin to flow.

from *The Triumph of Love*

I

Sun-blazed, over Romsley, a livid rain-scarp.

V

Obstinate old man – *senex*
sapiens, it is not. What is he saying;
why is he still so angry? He says, I cannot
forgive myself. We are immortal.
Where was I? Prick him.

VI

Between bay window and hedge the impenetrable holly
strikes up again taut wintry vibrations.
The hellebore is there still,
half-buried; the crocuses are surviving.
From the front room I might be able to see
the coal fire's image planted in a circle
of cut-back rose bushes. Nothing is changed
by the strength of this reflection.

X

Last things first; the slow haul to forgive them:
Chamberlain's compliant vanity, his pawn ticket saved
from the antepenultimate ultimatum; their strict
pudency, but not to national honour; callous
discretion; their inwardness with things of the world;
their hearing as a profound music
the hollow lion-roar of the slammed vaults;
the decent burials at the eleventh hour:
their Authorized Version – it has seen better days –

'nation shall not lift up sword against nation'
or 'nation shall rise up against nation' (a later
much-revised draft of the treaty). In either case
a telling figure out of rhetoric,
epanalepsis, the same word first and last.

XIII

Whose lives are hidden in God? Whose?
Who can now tell what was taken, or where,
or how, or whether it was received:
how ditched, divested, clamped, sifted, over-
laid, raked over, grassed over, spread around,
rotted down with leafmould, accepted
as civic concrete, reinforceable
base cinderblocks:
tipped into Danube, Rhine, Vistula, dredged up
with the Baltic and the Pontic sludge:
committed *in absentia* to solemn elevation,
Trauermusik, musique funèbre, funeral
music, for male and female
voices ringingly *a cappella*,
made from double string choirs, congregated brass,
choice performers on baroque trumpets hefting,
like glassblowers, inventions
of supreme order?

LI

Whatever may be meant by *moral landscape*,
it is for me increasingly a terrain
seen in cross-section: igneous, sedimentary,
conglomerate, metamorphic rock-

strata, in which particular grace,
individual love, decency, endurance,
are traceable across the faults.

LXXVI

At seven, even, I knew the much-vaunted
Battle was a dud. First it was a dud,
then a gallant write-off. Honour the young men
whose eager fate was to steer that droopy *coque*
against the Meuse bridgeheads. The Fairey
Swordfish had an ungainly frail strength,
cranking in at sea level, wheels whacked
by Channel spindrift. Ingratitude
still gets to me, the unfairness
and waste of survival; a nation
with so many memorials but no memory.

CXLIX

Obstinate old man – *senex
sapiens*, it is not. Is he still
writing? What is he writing now? He
has just written: I find it hard
to forgive myself. We are immortal. Where
was I? –

CL

Sun-blazed, over Romsley, the livid rain-scarp.

from *Speech! Speech!*

22

Age of mass consent: go global with her.
Challenge satellite failure, the primal
violent day-star moody as Herod.
Forget nothing. Reprieve no-one. Exempt
only her bloodline's *jus natalium*.
Pledge to immoderacy the outraged
hardly forgiven mourning of the PEOPLE,
inexorable, though in compliance,
media-conjured. Inscrutable Í call
her spirit now on this island: memory
subsiding into darkness, nowhere
coming to rest.

37

These I imagine are the humble homes
the egalitarian anti-élitist SUN
condescends to daily. Democracy
is in the voice – Churchill's or some other –
I cannot now hear; and the missing clue
WANHOPE: missing, that is, from the game
celebrity plays us for; not lost, since I
still seem to possess it. You too, Jack! –
know who I mean, eh? – poet and scholar
caught sashaying your shadow self. Say that
at normal walking speed, toes on the line.
Say: SURE SUCCESS OF RAP PAR FOR THE COURSE.

38

Do nothing but assume the PEOPLE'S voice,
its speaking looks of dumb insolence.
Xenophobic still the Brits are heroes
living as they have to – short-cuts, thwartings,
one circus act after another, the Powers
enlightened, vengeful: no darkness more
difficult of encounter. Show the folks
Caravaggio's FLAGELLATION – what's it worth? –
sensational, unfeeling. Award
damages for and against the press.
Why is the wreck still singing? All at once
to speak well of this – A FINE STORY!

57

Show you something. Shakespeare's elliptical
late syntax renders clear the occlusions,
calls us to account. For what is abundance
understand redemption. Who – where – are our
clowns WET 'N' DRY: will the photographs
reveal all? Só hate to be caught in mid-
gesture, you knów thát, noble CARITAS,
proud AMOR – pledge your uncommon thoughts.
See all as miracle, a natural graft,
as mistletoe ravelling the winter boughs
with nests that shine. And some recensions
better than thát I should hope.

from *The Orchards of Syon*

VII

Our fealties taken to be your places
of refuge and defence. Author? Author
is all one word, like Faculties. Can you
receive me? Unwise to make wise choices
too early. Incorrigible in any case
the human spirit or its spin-offs,
cogent, unreadable, and at some
personal cost a public nuisance:
not ineradicable but not soon
put down or uprooted. Best early flowering
or in the sere. Music arguably
not implicated in the loss of Eden,
held to its resolution. No
question an affirmation. Tell him he ís
alive – someone – and responsible. He may
respond to that, as to other electrodes,
as Lear to the sour-sweet music of viols,
as to some oils of unction or to Gospel.
Tune him to Gospel: *Over my head*
I hear music, music in the air. That
Gospel? Súre that Gospel! Thát sure
Gospel music in my head. Oh my sole
sister, you, little sister-my-soul,
this mý Gospel, thís sure músic in mý head.

XLVI

To love, determinedly and well, and to be
unfaithful: there should have arisen
particular broken forms to engage this;
brutish presentiments heavy as the sea
that rides from darkness onto a skirr
and pash of shingle. Montale, in *Finisterre*,
focused something, his eros, though I can't
quote him or even recall
clearly what he said of desire and absence
of the desired. Such is Eros, pupil
of the moon, with full corolla
presaging migraine; or, as I see it, self
rectifying vision indefinable.
Is anything out there? To love
determinately, to redispose
death in this strange body? Held by evidence
I say again: passion and inertia
overwhelm us, like a waste
surf compounding with its undertow.
Many waters cannot quench Phosphor.
See how it's done, plunderers
of subtext, caught flotsam, even of your own
eye-catching inane flare, these other words
borne out beyond your salvage, there as here.

L

Covenants, yes; outcries, yes; systemic
disorders like the names of rock-plants, yes;
right side for creativity, yes; and well
if none of ús fails our provision.
Go to the revivalists for vision,
the charismatic troupers. Planets
of alkali, no; a methylated cold
glow in the northern heavens that spells God
the encoder, no. Who is *long suffering
to us-ward*? Oh man! More sensual,
at times craven, clay our solicited
Maker must make do with. This means love
and fear, soul-sister, bounden by deed of gift,
by imputation and by adoption,
by sighs and groans – *uh-húh* –
to stay and sway us, as never before.
O never before heard preaching like it,
saving your presence, maestro, as it soars
spontaneous, by the book, the plenitude
of the oppressed, oppressive and upgathered.
Not condign here to bespeak reprobation,
to exhaust Egypt, rise from a dead sea.
H'm–h'm! Keep her hummin' Lord! The day
of Jubilo, though new to my programme.

LVIII

La vida es sueño, and about time;
about hanging in there, about my self,
my mind as it is, to be remembered,
regarding timegraphs: these I understand
as the nongrammatical speech of angels.
I mean, they're beyond grammar that reminds
us of our fall, and of hanging out there.
My mind, as I know it, I still discover
in this one-off temerity, arachnidous,
abseiling into a pit, the pit a void,
a black hole, a galaxy in denial.
Life ís a dream. I pitch
and check, balanced against hazard,
self-sustained, credulous; well on the way
to hit by accident a coup de grâce.
Intolerable stress on will and shall,
recovery of sprung rhythms, if not rhythm;
test of creation almost to destruction –
that's a smart line; it can survive me.
In denial not my words. I'm moving
blindly, all feelers out. Cosmic flare-wind
tilts the earth's axis, then returns us,
with our ears singing, our eyes rolled back,
mute, Atlantean.

from *Scenes from Comus*

1. THE ARGUMENT OF THE MASQUE

2

That we are inordinate creatures
not so ordained of God; that we are
at once rational, irrational, possessed by reason.

That this is no reason for us to despair.
The tragedy of things is not conclusive;
rather, one way by which the spirit moves.

That it moves in circles need not detain us.
Marvel at our contrary orbits. Mine
salutes yours, whenever we pass or cross,

which may be now, might very well be now.

5

Add that we're unaccountably held to account;
that we cannot make our short days add up
to the sum demanded. Add, that accountancy

is a chartered profession, like surveying;
that rectitude is a grand directive;
that righteousness has no known charter

and is not, generally speaking, in demand.
That there are immoderate measures in plenty;
that plenty is a term of moderation;

that moderation is by some used to excess.

6

That, in these latter days, language
is the energy of decaying sense;
that sense in this sense means *sensus communis*.

That common sense bids me add: not
all language. If power's fuelled by decay,
so be it – decay being a natural force.

Moral corruption is another matter;
I cannot get beyond pronouncing it
inertia of malevolence, or *pondus*.

This *pondus* has itself nothing to add.

7

That stale enlightenment exacerbates
the incoherence – ask me to explain –
profuse expediency that leaves us speechless,

wordless, even. Their words attack my throat
wordlessly. If it were silence to silence!
Silence is dealt defending a loved child

against incorrigible fact. Mute
suffering's a factor of countless decibels.
I see the pristine hammer hammer alarm.

I see it but I can hear nothing.

2. COURTLY MASKING DANCES

nello stile antico

18

This is a fabled England, vivid
in winter bareness; bleakly comforting,
the faded orchard's hover of grey-green.
We have come home, say, all is well between us.
Sharp-shining berries bleb a thorn, as blood
beads on a finger or a dove's breast pierced
by an invisible arrow to the heart.

26

The corrupter, the abuser, the liverish
ravager of domestic peace. The soi-disant
harmless eccentric. Nobody's harmless.
Neither is comedy. Maybe the polka
injured thousands. In this depleted time
revive me, take me to a blue
movie, hold my hand in the dark.

Improvisations for Jimi Hendrix

Somewhere a Queen is weeping
Somewhere a King has no wife

1

I am the chorus and I urge you
act messenger's idiom from Greek tragedy.
Get to know words like the gods'
inconstant anger.

Stand in for Pasiphaean bull,
Exquisite player of neumes!
Enlarge the lionized
apparatus of fucking.
Wacko falsetto of stuck pig.

You can vibe self-defector and know
how to project
Olympian light waves.

The show guitar melts like sealing wax.
It mutes and scalds. Your fingers
burning secrets.

Your legerdemain.

Extraordinary progressions chart
no standard progress.

Call guru noises to task.
There is no good ending admits fade-out.
By rights you shall have
top prize longevity
wiped as a gift.

2

Prime time, whole time, the planet's
run by toupée'd pinkoes: but not ruled.
Not even music rules.

What kind contortions fix hex-mind pyrewise?

Something unexplained – I exempt his music.

No huckster, then, dazed gambler with real grace,
saved possibility; and the hotel rooms
destroyed themselves.

3

Short-changed and on short time let us
walk óh-so óh-so with all new gods.
Showmen kill shaman, dunk parts in late

wag-chat's petty brine. I had a line all
set to go; a lien now. Even the shadow-
death cues further shadows. Take his hand,
Medea, if he can find it. *Lysergic*

also is made up Greek.

4

Sometimes the king of a forbidden country
has his entitlement, his lineage,
adorned by error.

Somehow a king delivers his true bride
in the perilous
marsh of childbirth and all three go safe.

Yes there is weeping and yes some find
the lost miracle and do not know it;

swagger royally, play the pretender
to sinking Atlantis,
drown in their star-dust. Some are reborn.

. . .

Somewhere the slave is master of his desires
and lords it in great music
and the children dance.

from In the Valley of the Arrow

3

My shadow now resembles my father's: cloth
cap flat-planted with its jutty neb
that prods the leaf-litter. Ineffectually.

What do they think of while they think of nothing?
Thinks: check pulse-rate as last animus
jerks home – spit, spat – *they* of course being *them*.

The finite mind transcends its finitude
with the contrivance of affinities,
on the great wheel that keeps time in suspense.

Dying's no let-up, an atrocious
means of existence: nobody saved;
no sign of ransom if you comprehend me.

Smug bastard.

4

Heart-stab memento giving a side-glimpse
of feared eternity – left at the kiosk –
as on a bright path you might catch the shadow
of your attacker.

Sun off shields in middle distance
and lidded water saurian-scaled.

Standing or going there is always pain;
the machinations of set injuries;
sentiment in collusion with itself.

The wild geese racket and mute swans proceed
in formal agitations round the lake.

Not all his days are this eventful.

    5

More than you know it's like dead trees that stay
the same, winter and summer – odds
on how he tells it – sheathed in samurai
mail of black ivy. At it again,

beata l'alma.

Unzipped and found addressing the smeared walls
of an underpass, crying not my
address, no more unnamed accusers,

self-dubbed natural thespian enacts
age, incapacity – judge the witnesses –
brings himself off to video'd provocation.

Pardon my breathing.

from *Pindarics*

14

Say Coriolanus fought from dark to dark,
a thing of blood; such as he told his mind
he could turn cities ashen, being empowered
by slow brain-worm to swift self-travesty;
bespoke *a lonely dragon in his fen* –
that sentimental – something more than huff –
and hitting wild accord, a douce of rage,
blood-tears by contract, servitor of guilt.
Shakespeare's gold-trading; mortgages; a name.

Stress here that Ces was exiled to twelve months
of dire self-catering at Brancaleone,
Musso's block-strutters pinned him in their charts
marked as tame dragon; this at worst was true;
decently wounded, asthma and cockroaches
and self-reproach. Alas they tortured Ginzburg
and Ginzburg died. That was another time.
I have some feeling for his widow's brusqueness.
Implicate wit to air-freshen the fact.

For Coriolanus there is no escape
in the sublime, in God, or melancholy,
no music for his state, no martyrdom,
no reconciling with the truth of things;
but, crazy-passive, a last mêlée of spite.

Citations I

This not quite knowing what the earth requires:
earthiness, earthliness, or things ethereal;
whether spiritus mundi notices bad faith
or if it cares; defraudings at the source,
the bare usury of the species. In the end
one is as broken as the vows and tatters,
petitions with blood on them, the charred prayers
spiralling godwards on intense thermals.

No decent modicum, agreed. I'd claim
the actual is at once cruder and finer,
without fuss carrying its own weight. Still
I think of poetry as it was said
of Alanbrooke's war diary: a work done
to gain, or regain, *possession of himself,*
as a means of survival and, in that sense,
a mode of moral life.

from In Memoriam: Gillian Rose

1

I have a question to ask for the form's sake:
how that small happy boy in the seaside
photographs became the unstable man,
hobbyist of his own rage, of hurt women.
You do not need to answer the question
or challenge imposture.
Whatever the protocol I should still construe.

2

There is a kind of sanity that hates weddings
but bears an intelligence of grief
in its own kind. There are achievements
that carry failure on their back, blindness
not as in Brueghel, but unfathomably
far-seeing.

3

Recap on words like compassion that I
never chanced in your living presence;
as empathy and empowerment.
I did not blunder into your room with flowers.
Despite the correct moves, you could have wiped me
in the championship finals of dislike.

4

Might you have responded to my question?
One will never know. You asked not to be
cheated of old age. No kidding, it is an
unlovely parley, although you

could have subdued it and set it to work,
met it without embracing. Edna
with her prosthetic jaw and nose
prevails over these exchanges.

.   .   .   .   .   .

11

A familiar rare type of resistance
heroine, like that woman, is required by justice.
Whether the omens are propitious or unpropitious
the Lysander takes off, heads south, the Maquis
line out the chosen ground, the landing-strip,
with their brave vulnerable fires.

12

Sometimes the Gestapo are waiting, sometimes not,
and she gets clear. But the odds are heavy.
The odds are heavy-set against us all
though medics call the chances symbiosis
in their brusque insolent manner that denies
self-knowledge as the sufferer, her formal agon:
that word you chose to use, a standard term
but not despicable in context of *Love's Work*.

13

Poetry's its own agon that *allows us
to recognize devastation* as the rift
between power and powerlessness. But when I
say poetry I mean something impossible
to be described, except by adding lines
to lines that are sufficient as themselves.

14

Di-dum endures formally; and the pre-Socratics.
Phocion rests in his lost burial-place.
Devastated is estuary; *devastation* remains
waste and shock. This ending is not the end,
more like the cleared spaces around St Paul's
and the gutted City after the fire-raid.
I find *love's work* a bleak ontology
to contemplate; it may be all we have.

from *The Daybooks I:*
Expostulations on the Volcano

45

It is All Souls' Eve and one damson tree
Stands as miser to its wiltering leaves.
The best of British, dumb-blind Samsonry,
Cleaves to those rots like rose-roots into graves.

Brisk wind off the Fens drags through evergreens,
Sets fruit trees to rapid, stiffish, motion;
More presences here sensed of the unseens,
The putting-by, pull of hibernation.

Qliphoth it is not: St Vigor's louvres
Visible now through stained autumnal mesh.
A commonplace of morning manoeuvres
Itself into such a splendour of trash

That I have come to stand at the house door,
Awkward with lame synergy, revelling.
Lawrence, who knew each creature by its spoor,
The dead by yet-tenacious hard dealing,

Vexed variously the spirit of place.
I name, according to drift's burden, grief
And things vestigial, like the gummy trace
Tugged from old damson bark, an amber quiff.

48

Jacob wrestling with the angel one thing;
With a ladder another. If the late
Writings are about grace and self-loathing
Tick the box; if comedy is your fate

Know how it strikes you. All could be sudden
Master-erasure or slow consignment,
Brutish beholdings tamed and beholden,
Obscure heart-splinter fleshed as truth's figment:

Craft-ingrown lace-maker of blitzed Ypres
As it might be; fable could up its bid.
Not as gift the rigged target of prayers,
Parachute-harness hung, still crucified.

I should mutter you blanked out with the fall
As we expected; but that you are now
Master of the small bribes, theatrical
Posings, wills, worthless disclosures at law.

If *Cairncross*, say, was *a strange bitter man*
Who could have done untold harm but didn't
By weirdest chance, if the next letter can
Yield you top score, who shall go unpardoned?

49

Time and light move simultaneously
In either direction: such is my view
Based on a vision that came painlessly
And liquorless as mostly I am now.

I say *painlessly*; but there stands belief
With things densely familiar. Time, great
Laden shuttle reduced to its begriff,
In which you and I, love, rue with Wyatt,

Against the whinge of pulsars; a pressure
Unimaginable; here recognized
And with charts to prove them. I am less sure
Of other measures anarchs have devised.

Clue me as to how we are immortal
Yet again. Yet again impulsive flares
From lourd sophistry, of misrequital;
Much as this causeless spin our lords and heirs

Have not forefashioned. Must we end with him,
This mortifying old man, his bent wits,
With the slow-dying spiral of his rhyme;
And with whatever else in judgement sits?

from *The Daybooks II: Liber Illustrium Virorum*

XXXVIII

Gauche poet does right by wronged general:
There is a lilt to that, it takes the truth.
In part you're Cincinnatus or de Gaulle;
One or the other, less likely both;
Famed as a holding spirit in the breach;
Brave scare emblazoned through the palimpsest;
Some call to readjust
The Ides of March;
The mob ranged in its dust
Crying the cost:
The slow trajectory
Of peace imploding victory.
So to this grave, this avenue; you have
The verdured gods, the flood, the architrave;
A marbled floor through which
The light may glitch
And run like wax; here turn
A torso or an urn;
The painted shadow-keel,
The ceiling-arch
A pool of nymphs wherein you sway and reel.

LIII

From that which is not relevant we draw
Appropriate lessons. Celebrating
King James for its approval rating
Is not on. You smile as if I were slow.
Ranter Joe's my man in his marginal
Costituency of faith; though much good
May it do me. He stood
Original
Sin on its scurfy head;
Election's goad
Prodding salvation's way
As he bellowed *coal!* from his dray.
Unreceived in the theme-park, folk museum –
How awkward there his presence, his *I am* –
He stands as when first roused
By God; though razed
Each nerve in his employ;
The status of his joy
Yielding no carbon date;
Unmenial
His hand upon the blank Mosaic slate.

from *The Daybooks III: Oraclau | Oracles*

14

Distant rain-draped slate flanks gleam like late snow
At high summer as the sun parades them,
  Cloud intermittently shades them,
  As our eyes interpret shadow;
    And the sheep are angled
Against the field walls that are quartz-spangled;
Celin bushes with raw wool-sprouts tangled;
Shadow supplanting shadow, Eryri;
The eagle glinting to its lost eyrie.

108

Novembering Wales, the flooded meadows
Pewter, lead-sheeting, briefly highlighted;
  Grand sog of red woods gold-leaf fretted;
  The road squeezed skywards from wrung Betws;
    Now the deep-held tremor
Of pelting gullies that are wisps in summer
Behind the stone house with the slate shimmer;
Again this homing, strangely-abrupt word,
Possessed domestication of your goad.

from *The Daybooks V: Odi Barbare*

XXVIII

Broken that first kiss by the race to shelter,
Scratchy brisk rain irritable as tinder;
Hearing light thrum faintly the chords of laurel
    Taller than we were.

Fear to have already the direst choosing,
Sixty years spent as by procrastination.
Answer one question, this is all I need, so
    Speeding denial.

Ancient question haunting the Platonist: can
Spirit ransom body, and if so could I
Rise again in presence of your devoting
    Sorrow to sorrow?

Quick, is love's truth seriously immortal?
Would you might think so and not be this other
Finally known only through affirmation's
    Failing induction.

What though, wedded, we would have had annulment's
Consummation early, and though in darkness
I could see that glimmerious rim of folly
    Lave our condition,

Had we not so stumbled on grace betimely
In that chanced day brief as the sun's arising
Preternaturally without a shadow
    Cast in its presence.

XLV

Here at full noon only endormant cloudscapes,
Active curtailed nerves of the earth-scarps braded,
Flense of some late glacier's vanished keel yet
    Cutting between them.

Sunning, selfblazoned, the great gorse conclamant
Rakes and reivers barrens; rebuilds burnt acres.
What requires my heart to acclaim its own well
    Set in the vistas?

If on some raw tangent I yet outlive you,
Late eccentric (why must we seem so formal?),
Begging something you had once said, *old age is*
    Not for the squeamish.

Once and always this is the merest memo.
I do not see us reabsorbed in nature.
Would you start back if I revamped this saying
    Very well show me?

This is what I signed for – *musicien français*
But in English – as when that time-eliding
Brief rhapsodic lento begins Debussy's
    Cello Sonata.

Throps a buzzard, lazily photographs his
Aerial scenics. Be a fool and say so:
Adamantine age set to melt in flames of
    Absolute longing.

from *The Daybooks VI: Al Tempo de' Tremuoti*

SEI MADRIGALI

To P. M. H.

88 (a)

Is it not strange that thou shouldst weep? So gravid
The sweetest song a burdening: the six
Metamorphoses, of violence and sex,
The sensuous oboe touched by sensual Ovid.

Pan pipes, the syrinx, the Orphic lyre;
The waters of the mere, reedy and full;
Poignant the false-relationed madrigal;
The hunter poised, the watcher with the lure.

88 (b)

The heron's flight out of the reeds is laggard
Yet still it climbs. You could have watched its slow
Navigation of the risen dawn,
Its neck drawn back, prehensilely long-legged,

But you were probably asleep, and I
Display too late my early grief. Too late
Pinions of holding lift and agitate.
The heron crests its high-reared heronry.

88 (c)

This keeping of delight makes to its strath.
As we must know it, the *perturbèd moon*
Which is the singular being and yet none
And of the sexual will its grief its graith,

Suffuses, broadens, rouses to subside.
Here too the archaic and reflective swan
Ploughs through its image before setting down.
The river-margins brim with each new tide.

88 (d)

So, solace without respite, as when, coursing through the ear, Italian lute-songs
With preciosities pluck at the heart-strings,
Thy studied dissonance, *crudel Amor*.

Caccini's *Amarilli* I would play
At school assemblies, a scuffed seventy-eight
Bucking the needle, churning sweet disquiet.
Our loves are dying, we have had our day.

88 (e)

What would I have us do, enshrine Sosostris'
Aria from that fey *Midsummer Marriage*,
Joyous transcendent threnos before mere age,
All-mastering strings quelling things queer, disastrous?

Somewhere within the extravagant gauche plot
Is our true-plight, misfathomed salutation.
If we should labour back against time's motion
Still distant are those lovers we were not.

88 (f)

What I have so invoked for us is true
As invocation. The Fibonacci range
Of numbers is a constant, like Stonehenge.
Like Ovid's book of changes to construe.

I can see someone walking there, a girl,
And she is you, old love. Edging the meadow
The may-tree is all light and all shadow.
Coming and going are the things eternal.

Toby Martinez
de las Rivas

Twenty-One Prayers for Weak or Fabulous Things

As snow falls, as the first snow of this year falls & falls
    beyond all light & knowledge, I pray for Rufus
corrupted by lung parasites: whose viscera is corrupted
    & whose eyes are uncorrupted by flitting about
in the weak light. I speak this prayer into the black sun.

Secondly, I pray for David, who watches his dead sister
    wandering the yard each morning, up and down,
a shadow of herself. I pray for all things that slough off
    their skins: for snakes, for cicadas & silkworms
set doggedly to branches & pent in the rush of the bush.

Thirdly, I pray for a babbling, drunk fisherman wearing
    no trousers, dredged from the Tyne, who swore
ever after that by singing to Cuthbert he was able to call
    pearly trout from the river, to throw themselves
from their element into his – & there they flop, gasping.

Fourthly, I pray for a war protester, picketing The Sage,
    whose banners are scattered with cluster bombs
like falling seeds having the real viridian sting of black
    pansies closing. I pray for all things that unfurl
& shadow the sun: its star-track raked in the winter sky.

Fifthly, I pray for the ghost of Rene, & the living ghost
    of Mary in the final blank stage of Alzheimer's
nodding, clucking & fumbling. I pray for the sunflower,
    petals tight about a face of seed, head nodding
imperceptibly nightward. It has arms, too: to hold itself.

Sixthly, I pray for a pair of yellowhammers on the wire
    who sing in English: *a little bit of bread & no cheese.*

These are the hills. Not the north. This is upland chalks.
    I pray for the wild ghost of Barry MacSweeney
which has a bird's throat & thrumming, elliptical wings.

Seventhly, I pray for the sparrow with a slashed tongue,
    who in Egypt wore a jackal's garish blunt head
& ferried dead children across the river, but in England
    he's a happy, fat fellow. I listen to his declining
brotherhood at Broadway: there is one fewer every day.

Eighthly, I pray for Jimmy, who touches Mary's hands,
    & looks into Mary's empty shell each Thursday,
also on her birthday & the slow mornings of Christmas.
    The filament burns out its solitary candlepower.
8 is the sign for the infinite & is also the sum of YHVH.

Ninthly, I pray for the boy lying out in the summer rain
    by the old pigeon lofts round the back of our house.
A boy: a father, but a boy too, failing to blink as globes
    of water drip into his eyes. To the moulting birds
he is a king at siege in the twinkle of his paraphernalia.

& I remember, one night when everyone was at the bar,
    opening up an eye in my wrist an inch & a half
back from the base of the thumb that glared left & right,
    then fixed itself faithfully on me, in my despite.
Kate, Kate. The morning gathered us in its white sheets,

white vestments, as when *Venus* in her burnished cleats
    drew out of Restronguet, the deep lines of linen
signalling cruelly from the shore as fog rose up like joy
    & a boisterous wind cuffed the heads off waves.
Tell this out, too: the curlew crying out over Culmhead.

Tenthly, I pray to the last few seconds of a cold August,
    when the world is silent, a sullen body of water
that brings the famished larva creeping to my fingertips,
    my tongue a water snail with soft horns forcing
its head from between my lips. Harp of dusk, & muscle.

My eleventh prayer is for Migdale checking the hooves
    of his sheep for rot peeling the hoof's heel, sole
& wall from their attachments to the foot: for the sheep
    like amputees lagging & nibbling at lung flukes
& brain worms: & some fall down in the clart, shaking.

My twelfth prayer is for the unfledged rooks overcome
    by ants beneath the high nests. For the membra
over the pods of their eyes. For the shine of their beaks
    & the orbit. For the boot I bring down on them.
Let me love best all these creeping things that creepeth.

My thirteenth prayer is to the ghost of Nicholas of Flüe,
    who saw the face of the Lord lacerated with fury,
& whose own face was fixed into a mask by that vision.
    The faint shapes of his children, flinching away.
Today even the little sparrow cannot bear to look at me.

My fourteenth prayer is for you, Isa, altered by distance.
    I see your heart, & it has the shape of the winter
cherry convulsing in the gale. Arterial web of branches,
    blossom battered off, acquiescence in the bough.
But mine is a bird fixed in the canopy – a false lapwing.

Sometimes, when we touch, you subtly shift your body
    ten degrees to the right or left – so it is your hip
or thigh, & not your genitals which shiver against mine:

TOBY MARTINEZ DE LAS RIVAS

we do not stand dovetailed, as the beating wing
should to the physicality of lift. Or the wall to its brace.

My fifteenth prayer is for the recoiling bee that I found
in the allotment, like a small aeronaut slumped
into the burst spars of his machine. He thumped his sting
once into the sodden ground to vent his temper
& is free to go. A cold season gathers itself in the earth.

And did I tell you about Burgess the miner, who tossed
the body of his daughter into the gut of the well
at Watercombe & married her stepmother in the woods:
he was caught out by the deadlight that winked
above the shaft: & a sheep rustler spied her down there.

Here they call a deadlight a spunky, the ghost of a child
that catches & flares above a tract of still water.
On Midsummer they gather at church to meet the souls
of the freshly buried, & invite each one to swell
their companies: but some of these I blame on cider.

My sixteenth prayer is for the drunk staggering through
a shattered gate in Thomas Bewick's tail-piece:
after the merganser ascetically rearranging its plumage,
after the mute swan riding from its harbourage
like a troubled schooner. & in the sky – a double moon.

My seventeenth prayer is to the memory of Christopher
Smart kneeling in a torrent of bees at Staindrop
to pray, or cutting the Song to David into the bare page
of a wall with a claspknife & a splinter of glass,
& with his fingertip rubbing charcoal into the scratches.

My eighteenth prayer is for the glass ghosts of Leopold
    & Rudolf Blaschka, combinations of moonlight
& organ, slight tendrils of glass teasing out their quarry
    by tentacle & night vision. The Scyphomedusa
flows above us, a star in a doomed pod or constellation.

My nineteenth prayer is for the one who kept his watch
    on the stair the night we brought the bairn back,
the iron of whose glare counteracts supernatural malice.
    After the owl & dragon, he is the most puissant
& canny of all living beasts. The devil cannot pass him.

My twentieth prayer is for the wind sobbing in the haw,
    & the lamb that lurches through the Pentateuch.
Tobe, Tobe, you have called him here to face the music
    & be thrust face down in the beck, shorn of life,
the tongues of water whispering its lineage into his hair.

Last, I pray for the makers of prayers, which are poems
    we say to ourselves in the hard times, dry times,
cold times. In tenements, in tower blocks, in the locked
    tin caskets of our hearts. In the darkness, falling
& falling like snowflakes beyond all light & knowledge.

Three Illustrations from *Blake's Europe: A Prophecy*

FRONTISPIECE

Kneeling in *contrapposto*, the shoulders and arms
Twist against the swelling vertical axis of the left leg.
Muscles set in shadow and raucous, oppositional light.
This is one aspect of the ideal nude: arrayed as man,
Pre-democratic and wholly local, wholly sufficient.
The borrowed contortions, the splayed web of fingers
Or wind-blasted hair raddled with age, feebly white.
Heaven adorned with fire, darkness divided against
Itself where he leans to set the bright stars and the law.
Delicate sash of eyelids half closed in concentration.
And what this posture connives with is what is in us,
Is what we are: inexorable, self-willed bowing down.

PLATE VIII

Hold yourself to yourself, my lost and keening one.
Beyond this room, and this fire, and this infant body
Stretched in abject stillness on the floor, lies nothing
But the failed State, arming itself against consolation.
What does she want, this duchess, in the blue lustre
Of her robes, if not to tax you to death and eat you,
A ring of white pearls at her beating heron's throat
As the cruel and oblatory smoke ascends in clouds?
Who can doubt, now, that he foresaw and foreheard
The full range of tragedy: Passchendaele and Omaha,
Torrejón de Ardoz, Guernica: that in my grandfather's
Throat seemed the vocables of a paradisal language?

PLATE XVII

Jerusalén. Of which the stylobate at extreme left
Is surely an outrider, the suburbs of the Holy City.
Look at the purpose in the eye of this tall, naked boy,
His right leg planted on the bottom step, his lover
Upon his shoulders, his massive torso twisted to drag,
From the following flames, his bairn, his daughter.
This is the ideal nude: not arrayed in flesh, but really
Flesh: sprung from earth, newly risen, individuated.
Beneath whose bare foot the secularity of stone rests
Its cold and dependable mass, begging to be shaped.
He shall make of his own arms a fold, that the gale
May pass them by, the fire not bite them with its teeth.

Poem, Three Weeks After Conception

The sky will be shaped like a bow when you crane your neck to pray into it. Roofless, but not burned. Though black, spangled.

Your hair will be the white spray at High Force, teeth pebbles in the vent.

You will escape the ogre of psoriasis that lives on the knees, elbowcaps, genitals and face.

For you the stars have already locked into place.

For you the blue coltsfoot in the allotment will be an electrical wonder.

The Red Kite, wolf and bear will return to the borders in numbers.

You will be buried in a country far away, a country like home, of absolute rainfall.

Beneath a late moon, unfurling.

You shall witness the domination of Jerusalem.

The capsize of London.

I pray that I will never hit or humiliate you,
for whom the best wine in the world will be pressed in Kent.

Who will live to see supermarkets dictating military policy to governments.

Our Lady of Gateshead, watch over us.

Things I Have Loved

The Flea, principally,
pronounced *Flay*.

Smart, who disliked clean linen,
whom Johnson would as lief pray with as anyone.

Paper aeroplanes like prayers in childhood, winged, rising, risen.

Headflare in multi-directional light, that Blackdown morning
the lamb was born, dead, beside his sister.

XXVI March,
the jute-sack and the shovel, as if by magic.

My never-to-be-born daughter, of the House of Míro Quesada.

How her body bucked like a beast dragged by its neck from the holt
when I touched it as instructed.

Each breath, a mist or brief rapt element, swept up,
escaped.

Fenlight, shivering in its seat.

Blackdown Song

In front of the gate whose tubes hummed in the wind
like owls hooing each other across a dark field, Isabel,
was the firepit's tract of soot-soft & snow-white ashes.

It went deeper than you knew, after years of bonfires,
dusks when sightly wings of paper flared in a woosh
of sparks & ghosted into darkness like minor stars.

Beyond the singing gate lay the dark field which ate
the bodies of lambs & threw up the bleached fans
of pigeon wings: the grass grew red in those places.

I dug the pit with a shovel & scooped bucketloads
to feed my father's garden which drew down silver
mouthfuls of ash & the tangled brown potato haulms.

All the while the gate hummed tunelessly in the wind:
tunelessly, but with range: high & low, long & short,
disconnected, artless, dumb life struggling into song.

I struck so reckless, Isabel – hot, one-handed, peeved,
& clanged a rock that hung in earth as consciousness
is said to inhere in the self, the self to hang in the body.

High, low, long, short. My arms went dead, a dazed bird
burst from my skull – the rock humped, deaf to the blow.
A brilliant ringing in the blade secured itself to that axis.

Père

Nothing before or since so clear as this: the windshield
iridescent, the heads of sanfoin in blazing brightwork,
a little Duke of Burgundy recumbent on whitlow-grass
sumptuous in its slashed doublet of dun-and-tangerine.
I might be betraying him the simplicity of his pleasure,
this man I rarely knew unguarded, his binoculars tilted
to the silhouettes of Phantoms like flies on the horizon.
Far-sighted, in the manner of Père Chérubin d'Orléans.
Half-leant against the searing bonnet in a frazzled shirt,
in old blue boxer-shorts with the cock-hole stitched up.

Untitled

Poetic space here signifies *page* in London, a language
I only half speak. Ah, Blanchot, these heaving galleries,
rats in tortoiseshell nerd-glasses, reproduction Jacobite war-
apparel and spadrilles, pathetically self-indentured.
Re-imagine all the bitter works of redemption as cheap
aesthetic, historical suffering assuaged as literary trope,
Purcell's death chants piped over the duct-taped rubble,
and you glimpse hell as it really is: not swathed in fires,
but overflowing with diversion, its connate bankruptcy
& anguish – or whatever it denotes, this tenacity of loss.

Testament

Look, it is March as it always is, the disordered spectra
rainbowed in wet asphalt or else invisible, hi-vis power
walkers buried in music jerking their heads defensively in
time, pitbulls barely tethered, the clotted buds of ash
groping to-usward, salvation's blind or suffering intent.
Also in time: the supernumerary rainbows stanchioned
in glassy shallows overflying both Huish and Langport
reassert their covenant: are, were, overbearingly bright
signals of conviction, promissory against black nimbus.
As Neruda's *violeta*, self-collapsing. In *corolla of rage*.

Misereatur

Psoriatic bough snow, dessicate blossom reconfigured in a vortex, transluminous grass-heads blighted with it, the muzzled Alsatian whining through her death mask at wasps: in bitterness the almonds are rigging the hills. That I have kept a tiny and concealed speck of myself innocent through sexual betrayal, through punishment, that I am in my marrow a physical coward, I find hard to reconcile with any notion of mercy or assuagement justly made: nor do I see what authority this disclosure holds in nature, beyond a plaintive and facile catharsis.

Woodbury

Óh, Óh, Óh, the fritillary sunning itself on nightshade,
photovoltaic fan of the wing-array twitched open shut
open in spasmodic adoration, chalk radiant in furrows,
the world aglow, preparatory, not yet in conflagration.
Unbroken pa, my balsawood chuck glider is crowning
the thornbush, ungetdownable, the sun amassing itself
in the leading edge, wedged by the wind, driven upon.
God, how the brain beats stripes out of itself, the body
unsalveable, stunned in its tree. I am heartily sorry for
my fault, my offence. All that is in me spells its dread.

Hurry

And Purgatory not as excarnation, not as final theosis,
but here and inwardly among the penultimate realities,
the stillness that presages παρουσια, the widening eye
of the storm that shall churn lime leaves to fish-scales,
narratives and counter-narratives in abrupt contention,
weathervanes spun wailing through their many points.
Oh pa, behold yr son in the dazzling mirror of his self-
regard, flung through that glass, unanchored, as chaff.
I had a suit to plead: but so much of the summer wind
tilts in my mouth, I cannot set one word down straight.

(clouds)

,   ,
                    ,
    ,
              ,
          ,   ·
        ,   ,
      ,
                    ,
                  ,   ·
  ,   ,   ,
      ,   ,
                                          ,
                ,   :
              ,
            ,   ·

(clouds)

from *Black Sun*

littleness has come, and a light betrays the walls of your Sodom? I summoned my heartland under the sun's blinding rim. Nothing. No Lux Aeterna. Will you know when the time for your

Hunting Kestrel, Danebury

Here is the ghost of a child I once knew
still playing among the withering harebells
& the gorgeous *moue* of the fairy flax.
I look beyond his bare golden head
to the kestrel that quarters the ramparts
& see a semblance of absolute love,
absolute mercy – at least a baffling, wild
joy – that, at least – in the watchfully poised
javelin of the head, the rapidity
of hér stoop & strike, hér failure, hér re-
lofting, the gaze that hungers into the spindle
without end: whose flowers are blood-red,
whose roots drive down among the lost chieftains.
A lonely god waits for us in the earth.

Intimate Portrait I/for S. N.

The starkly intimate moment you pee
in front of me for the first time – the glass
vague with condensation as your eyes
frame themselves in the mirror's stare.

Turning, I catch a look I've not seen
before – half apologetic, half exposed,
both at ease & on edge as you compose
yourself & undo the black ritual gown.

A deftness in you, neither innocence
nor calculation – more a sharp instinct
for the complicity that grants assent,
your vulnerable strength a clairvoyance

as you wind the paper round your hand,
then draw it between your legs & stand.

To a Metropolitan Poet

One day, I shall have to give an account
of *my* self with my knees couched
in dirt & the great cities tumbling like stars.
If not to hím, then to that portion of *my*
self that holds the rod & sits in judgement.
Out in the snowstorm, & the lake
like a field of burning heather, beautiful.
Christ, I can't stand those popinjays,
so deep in theory, so ostentatiously tolerant.
Always wanting to interrogate
shit or excavate shit, when what they mean
is read shit. This is so fucking point-
less, *Tobe*. You are not theirs, finally, or even
hís, that sees beauty where no other can.

Diptych: At Matfen / Address to my Daughter

Faded kingdom: the swallows bear their blued
bodies low over the green. They are grace
itself, snatching a raindrop from the air,
mowing a swathe through clouds of *Diptera*.
Nothing will rescue this from the city –
they come so arch, my generation,
so French with irony, *mwah*, *mwah*, *mwah*,
up for the weekend with endless profile
updates: me with a deerhound, me at the shoot,
me with a glorious dead light rising
in the eastern sky that is the moon casting
its gaze of deep anxiety between
the crowns of the beech trees, the river's thick
oils at midnight running with white fire.

Heri et hodie ipse et in saecula

Always the same. Whether I hold or whether
I do not, the centre does not wither –
it stays & stays through each changing season:
'. . . no variableness, nor shadow of turning . . .'
In us there is a turning: here, in these
collapsing bodies, in these minds, these hearts
like the swallow switching its aim between
targets, its manifold inconstancies
reaching out in despair to touch nothing
but the world's own bleak mutability.
Our beautiful & tender words – these, too,
are failing. Between the salon leftists
& the slaughterhouse of capital,
keep your wild hope in salvation's blindness.

Crucifixion with Dragonfly

Now the dragonfly breaks through the grey
shell of its body on a stalk of mace
& climbs into the world on that burnt black
flowerhead bobbing in the pretty wind.
The river flows, her deep dark oils & swirls
swell up & slide away; whose waters
shadow little depths; whose thin green weeds
unfurl their hair like a lost Ophelia.
There is a rainbow rising slowly through
the multiple facets of his single eye,
a wind that dandles the white of his wings,
a blind & burning cloud upon the hill.
He dries – his Arctic blues & molten golds
solidify around copper lamé.

In *Corpus Hypercubus* I cannot see
if the curled palms are really pierced by nails,
or if the crown of thorns still sits atop –
jauntily atop – the unrefusing head.
Hé has gone free of that dread assemblage;
there is only the beauty of the body
released back to the infinite peace of space,
& the sky blackening over Port Lligat.
No time redounds there – we, watching, are time
incarnate: breaking & broken, suffering
all things between the sea's distant breath
& the stare of the Magdalene until
our final cry that is a cry of pain
shatters the night with its *Laudate Dominum*.

Crucifixion, August, Lullington

Here are the crucified: I know some of them.
Some are being crucified as I speak.
& all, little daughter, step in their turn
to that sorrow that blossoms in the crown.
Are these, Love, the εἴδωλα of History –
the threshing floor in Matthew three twelve,
or a memory of no memory
where the dead instruct the living in hope
& these children genuflecting before
the golden statues begin their journey
into the same ignorance I know
so intimately, those familiar terrors
where the great blind god is a god of death,
& the image is always broken?

I have dreamed that body a thousand times,
the death that rolls across it an eclipse,
a black sun fringed with burning coronae.
In whose self-denial the bleak orbit
of a whole culture adapts itself to hope,
& more than hope – to history, worlds beyond this,
knowledge, carnality, love, joy, the dawn
that breaks upon the city of the dead.
I do not hate the world; I know it
a thin wish that each small thing be restored
to itself in final reconciliation,
the swallow at Lullington re-angling her wings
among dandelions in the yard at dusk –
my children, too, step up from the wreckage.

from Titan/All Is Still

Lord,
I shall lie down in the burning heather
is belief, like love, first a touch, a feeling,
an inclination toward rightness?
But I have known – known – myself right so
many times & been so, só wrong.
Is it a mode of dying? Of benediction?
Acceptance of suffering?
                                It is Benediction.
I am ill. There is a candle in the dark,
& I am standing at the rim of the candlelight
behind James Hickey. James Hickey
who had a script I would have killed for,
that I sweated to copy – fluent & expressive
in turquoise ink they only tolerated
for him; whose voice singing 'O come,
O come' held a scale of clarity & completion
that was emptiness, self-extinction:
perfect. James Hickey, as thick as muck,
barely able to long-divide, or parse, who gave
not one high fuck for poetry or English.
Yes, he was beautiful. I have hated beauty.
Lord, when will I sit at yóur left hand

> *Estoy en un calaboso*
> *lleno de abominaciones,*
> *ya me suben, ya me bajan*
> *a tomar declaraciones*

in the snowstorm? & the lake like a field
of burning heather: beautiful? I forget
which book it is, & who, where one of the dead
looks up through the fire & parabolas
of smoke as if from the sewer of a bombed

TOBY MARTINEZ DE LAS RIVAS

village to see his counterpart in the story
looking down at him from heaven
with no sense of pity, for justice forbids it.
Who? Father Abraham? Dives?
The other Lazarus? Lord, I am ill again.

* * *

Pillar of Fire

How far have we fallen? Do we keep falling?
Resisting as we fall, reaching out
in the dark to those falling about us? Some
we dig our fingers into, fall faster with
them – in pain – some we embrace
&, turning their faces towards our own,
with eyes closed, with mouths passionately
riven, arrest. That is the grace we have.
That is our *violencia* or *redención*.
That is the grace that is in us, in the (*clouds*),
not knowing & not given to know.
Oh, where are you? Were you there? Did
I not see you? Did I fall past you
in the darkness, the smoke pouring upwards?
Among post-it notes & memos fluttering
down like snow; among desks &
burning tech? Did I reach out? Did I touch
you with my fingers? Did you feel, &
were you consoled? At Jericho,
falling from the towers? Falling through
the (*clouds*), did I console your body,
falling? Did I love your body with the smoke
pouring upwards, seeing nothing, but still
loving your body as the trumpets rang?
As the walls fell outwards & the towers
collapsed through their own base-
ments with a shout? As all the people cried
out with one voice, falling & falling?
All crying out with one voice in the (*clouds*),
not knowing & not given to know,
the whole nation falling, & crying out?

& is the Lord the pillar of fire that burned
the priests of Baal, or is the Lord
the little cloud the size of a fist that hove
up on the horizon & it rained, at last,
after forty days & nights – or was it years –
anyway, it was súch a long time, Lord?
Lord, it is súch a long time since it rained.
& was it English rain, ambivalent
& gorgeous, the high beeches just visible
through it all, their leaves trembling
as if in a fever, & Israel from the borders
of Egypt to the valley of Goshen
a smear in the rain as Joshua tilteth his head
to hear the Lord speak that spake
from a deep (*clouds*) the will of Joshua
when he smashed Hebron & Ai?
When he smote Lachish with the edge
of his sword & the moon stood still
in the valley of Ajalon because he told it to?
When he burned Hazor & the seven kings
he hanged each from (*its*) own tree
for having looked at him with (*its*) faces
full of mala leche o algo, faces full
of bad milk or something, that was só
mighty & righteous in the Lord?
As later Ehud would come unto Eglon
king of Moab who *was* a very fat man &,
finding him in his summer parlour,
would say, 'I have a message from God
unto thee . . .' & when all that stood
by him had gone out, would lock the doors
& with his left hand draw a dagger
from his thigh of, what, about a cubit length
that he had girded under his raiment,

& thrust it in his great fat belly.
& his great fat belly was só fat, & the arm
of Ehud só mighty the haft would go in
after the blade, & the fat of Eglon
close about it with a slap as he knelt down
on his knees & the dirt came out. *Lord,*

* * *

Commentary: Matthew 19: 23-26

I have cut a hole in *my* body to see what
is there; knelt down on *my* knees
in the kitchen & hallowed the dirt beneath
the refrigerator. Like the king
when they took his children from him
& the wind was blowing in Gilboa
I have cut a hole in *my* body to see what is there,
& what is there is a red eye
struggling to open – what is there is a rent
vagina they will have to sink the long
needles of anaesthesia into,
sighing carefully to themselves & murmuring
¡Ay, qué cosa! ¡Qué cosa! Oh, what
a thing, what a thing.
That they will have to bind with staples
& a needle dragging fine strong black thread
in its wake like a mother pulling
her children down the street
crying *Oh, what a thing! What a thing*
are my children! Like fine strong black thread
tying me to the past & tying the wound
of me closed about itself. &
like fine strong black thread tying me
to the future which is coming down the road
emptying the gardens of colour.
Suburban gardens that glow with a deep inner
tranquility, with false cherubs peeing
on rocks & the dense magnoliae.
¡Ay, qué cosa! ¡Qué cosa!
Oh, what a thing, what a thing.
What a thing is a needle with its own eye

full of fine strong black thread.
On one side of it is the world & on the other
is heaven, & what a thing heaven is –
¡Mira, qué cosa! ¡Ay, qué cosa mas bonita!
So cold. So high & translucent. Cabinets & beds
stacked up as if in neverending audit &
the shapes of people visible in it
like people in a great city working behind glass
in a tower whose battlement is in the clouds.
¡Ay! What a thing is a (*clouds*),   , &
what kind of (*clouds*), & when, & in which light –
between whom, in relation to whom, &
whose & why & whereunto. & what a thing is David,
whose anger was like the coming of a (*clouds*),
who was King, who smote Abimelech
the son of Jerubbesheth. No, whó
smote Abimelech the son of Jerubbesheth?
Did not a woman cast a piece
of millstone upon him from the wall,
that he died in Thebez?
And when the mourning was past he fetched her
to his house, & Uriah the Hittite
was dead also. *Qué cosa. ¡Ay, qué cosa!* Oh, what
a thing is desire, & the man that has
desire in him, like a wasp in its dark holt,
like a black sun, like a throne with the (*clouds*)
upon it. Like a white moth. Like
the winds in the grass in the nearness & privety
of our sorrow,   , when rain starts
over the hill, the turquoise flares of lightning
striking the birch in triumph, & a flame
in the (*clouds*) deep in her torn leaves & Oh,
when I think thereupon there is such
súch singing & súch rich music in my head!

The great Saint-Saëns rumbling
away, & a trumpet going *tararí tarará* as
it is written the trumpets sounded at Jericho as the walls
collapsed outward & Joshua danced crying, '
I am the end.
I am the end of all things & all things end
in me. Galillee & love & shooflies & the stars.
In the closing of my eyes is the closing
of all things, & the great cities fall
down in them like snow.'

ACKNOWLEDGEMENTS

For material included in this selection the following grateful acknowledgements are made: to Rowan Evans for his poems from *returnsongs* (Wide Range, 2012), *freak red* (Projective Industries, 2015), *ODE RHIZOME MOUNTAIN SONG* (Moot Press, 2016) and *cante jondo mixtape* (If a Leaf Falls Press, 2017); to Jeremy Hill on behalf of the Literary Estate of Geoffrey Hill for poems from *Selected Poems* (Penguin, 2006); to Oxford University Press for Geoffrey Hill's poems from *Broken Heirarchies: Poems 1952–2012* (2013); and to Faber & Faber for Toby Martinez de las Rivas's poems from *Terror* (2014) and *Black Sun* (2018).

Other poems by Rowan Evans were first published in *Cambridge Literary Review*, *Halfcircle*, *Moot*, and *Reliquiae*; 'charm / vision' was first printed by letterpress as a folding diptych for Moot Press (2014).

FURTHER NOTES ON ROWAN EVANS'S POEMS

'rains' quotes Psalm 104, verse 32, in the King James version of the Bible.

The epigraph for 'A METHOD, A PATH' is from John Clare's poem 'Woodpecker's Nest', composed 1832–7.

cante jondo mixtape responds to Federico García Lorca's *Poema del Cante Jondo* (1931) and to Jack Spicer's *After Lorca* (1957).

'Envoys' quotes phrases from Maurice Merleau-Ponty's *Phenomenology of Perception* (1945) and Samuel Beckett's radio play *Embers*, first broadcast in 1959.

freak red misquotes the first line of Basil Bunting's *Second Book of Odes* (1964–75).

'Stems (1)' quotes phrases from Antonin Artaud's *The Theatre and its Double* (1938), translated by Mary Caroline Richards (Grove Press, 1994).

15:44 is the text for a performance and film collaboration with digital artist Maisie Newman. It was first commissioned by Mercy and Penned in the Margins for the EVP Sessions, Shoreditch Town Hall Basement, November 2015. The film was published online in *Datableed*, Issue 6 (2015). The poem quotes 1 Corinthians 15, verse 44 in the King James version of the Bible and phrases from T. S. Eliot's poem 'The Hollow Men', part IV (1925).

'charm / vision' quotes the first of the *Duino Elegies* (1923) by Rainer Maria Rilke, translated by J. B. Leishman (Penguin, 1964).